EXPLODED VIEW

OBSERVATIONS ON

READING, WRITING

AND LIFE

EXPLODED

Jean McKay

DRAWINGS BY *Roxanna Bikadoroff*

VIEW

DOUGLAS & MCINTYRE

VANCOUVER/TORONTO

Douglas & McIntyre Ltd.
2323 Quebec Street, Suite 201
Vancouver, British Columbia V5T 4S7

Canadian Cataloguing in Publication Data
McKay, Jean, 1943–
    Exploded view

    ISBN 1-55054-841-7

    1. Bikadoroff, Roxanna, 1964– II. Title.
PS8575.K287E96 2001   C818'.5407   C00-911486-6
PR9199.3.M3236E96 2001

Editing by Barbara Pulling
Cover and text design by Peter Cocking
Cover photograph by Eric Tucker/Tony Stone Images
Printed and bound in Canada by Friesens
Printed on acid-free paper ∞

We gratefully acknowledge the financial support of the Canada
Council for the Arts, the British Columbia Ministry of Tourism, Small
Business and Culture, and the Government of Canada through the
Book Publishing Industry Development Program (BPIDP) for our
publishing activities.

This book was written in the

intricate shadow cast by the departure

of Yo, Lung, and Stefan.

May they be at peace.

AUFFEURENSPRAXIS

I wish this word started with a different letter.
I don't want to begin with a disquisition.

I'd rather start slow and simple, with a clear
image. A young girl, maybe fourteen, saunter-
ing back through the woodlot in late summer.
She loosens the waistband of her skirt and fills
her underpants with crabapples. Walks through
the meadow, up the hill to the lone oak tree.
Lies down on her back in the long grass.

There's a warm wind. The branches of the
tree above her sway and pull at the trunk.
White clouds boil in the sky, the meadow-grass
is alive with snaking currents chasing down
the hillside. She lies in the middle of it, feeling
the nubbly pressure of apples packed between
her legs. The sun beats onto her face and her
outstretched arms. She's ready for something,
but she can't decide what. She thinks it might
be the voice of God. Burning bush/flaming
oak, her upbringing has been relentlessly

Protestant. But she's been through Grade 10 Health, so she also suspects it might be lust. It doesn't occur to her that they could be the same thing. She rolls onto her stomach, thrusts her pelvis into the apples, into the ground, feels the prickly meadow-grass on her outflung bare arms.

Let's leave her there, riding the crest of her ideological dilemma, and get down to business: auffeurenspraxis. It's primarily a question of intent. Tucked into the front end of *Grove's Dictionary of Music,* along with acciaccatura and appoggiatura (another pair of dualisms, like stalagmite and stalactite, or soffits and fasciae, that I can never tell apart). Auffeurenspraxis is the art of performing music as the composer intended. And what a can of worms that study has dumped onto our heads. Did they use vibrato in Bach's time? What would Mozart think of the synthesizer? If Beethoven had had access to the contemporary longer keyboard, would the sixteenth-note passage at bar 43 of the first movement of his Piano Sonata Opus 14, No. 2

have risen to the upper notes as it does later in bar 169, when it appears in a different key? Research, re-creation, it's all vexed and interesting, two poles of the territory represented on the one side by the Purists, and on the other by Who Gives a Shit? And, standing somewhere in the middle, is Of Course It Matters, but Not with a Pickle up your Butt. A cooler and wiser head.

Picture a winter's evening in 1782 in a drawing room in Leipzig. A gathering of people making music. They've arrived on foot (sidestepping the sewage in the gutters) or in carriages pulled by horses. Heat comes from a fireplace. The music they read is handwritten. The phone doesn't ring to interrupt them; no one's beeper goes off. But some things would be the same as they are today. Bathroom breaks. Phrasing regulated by the need to breathe. Fingerboards suddenly slippery from the sweat of hot flashes.

When my kids were small I was living in Wales. Christopher Hogwood (Mr. Auffeurenspraxis himself) came down from London to conduct a week-long workshop: choir, orchestra, presentations on "the history of ornamentation" and "instruments of the baroque era." People are amazed, when I tell them about it now. "Christopher Hogwood? Really? It must have been wonderful!" Well, I guess it was. Wonderful. I'll grab at any opportunity to play in an orchestra. I ran into him in Singleton Park late one afternoon. I was wheeling a pram, wearing a yellow miniskirt, singing, to the great amusement of the baby, "We all live in a yellow submarine." It was that year, whenever it was, Beatles topping the charts. We smiled at each other, Christopher and I. I recall that encounter better than the workshop itself. As I say, I still can't remember the difference between appoggiatura and acciaccatura.

Can this be possible? Can there have existed an incarnation of myself who wore miniskirts to the park? Evidently. Do I still know who Christopher Hogwood is? Sure. Does he still know who I am? Of course not.

So it plays itself out, this question of intent. I tend to think about it more when I'm reading, particularly student stuff. What is he getting at here? Does she mean me to think . . . ? On what windswept island, shrouded in what exquisite draperies, do they sit, sending out these glistening messages from their hidden hearts? What net do they imagine I'll be using to catch them?

What, for instance, did you make of the young girl with her pants full of crabapples? I wasn't intending titillation, although god knows it's an evocative image. But what am I trying to tell you? What are you picking up? What gossamer thread of comprehension is transmitted, by the touch of my pen on the paper, and received by your eyes from the page? We both have hearts, of that I can assure you.

BLESSING

I stood in the wind, unaccompanied, at the
starboard rail of the *Thomas Rennie.* As ferry
rides go, the Toronto Island run is a modest
one, but I embraced the nautical terminology.
I was in that kind of mood. The smallest slap of
water on galvanized hull was enough to get
me going. "A wet sheet and a flowing sea,"
I thought, "a wind that follows fast."

I was afloat. Gull-cries rendered my rib
cage both fragile and incandescent. Naiad,
Woman of the Deep, Elemental. My nose ran
but I cared not.

Suddenly before me, on the deck, there was
a crawling baby. Concern jolted me out of the
mythical. Her parents were nearby, smiling
and alert, so I slid back into my ethereal watery
self. I was was being approached by a very
young specimen of a complicated land species.
Her little knees, her little palms, worked away
to gain purchase on the oiled planking. She

arrived at my leg. She stopped. She lay her head down on my foot, sighed, and went to sleep.

My heart lurched. I stood there in the wind and every organ in my body, every system, conspired to become the perfect bed. My blood-stream murmured a lullaby, counterpoint to the ground of drumming engines.

The *Thomas Rennie* docked at the Island, the baby's father picked her up and bore her away. I walked onto land. My foot has since gone many miles, bearing the gentle weight of her slumber.

The raccoons have had more of the corn this
year than I have. It's the first time I've grown
corn, four rows, a modest patch. When I was
a kid, helping my dad sow corn, he always said,
"Three seeds to a drill: one for the hoe, one
for the crow, and one to grow." This spring I
ignored that, just planted with the simple faith
I always plant with, and it all came up. I didn't
figure on the raccoons.

Now I'm pulling out the stalks, dry and
rustling, and the mantra that's been the under-
current of my thoughts surfaces: "Choppy
voilence, choppy voilence." What *is* this?

After my dad died I wrote a book about him,
set him gently down on the page. I described
my mother, cleaning out the corn in the garden
while he was being cremated, using a hoe with
choppy violence. When I read the manuscript
over I found a typo, *voilence*, and I couldn't get
rid of it. I corrected it, but each time I made

9

a new draft it reappeared, my fingers more
accustomed to the other order of those vowels,
from words like soil, toil, spoil.

The stubborn repetition of this mantra in my
brain, I realize, is due to more than the activity
of cleaning out the corn. This was the season
when he died; the waning light is bringing it
back. Voilà. Discovery. Choppy discovery. And
here I am all this time later, being required to
lay him to rest yet again.

After his funeral, I played the old Methodist
hymns on the fiddle in the twilight beside a
river, the cooling air taking the sound beyond
landscape, taking him across to Jesus. When the
roll is called up yonder he'll be there. It's not
a heaven I'd choose for myself, but I was helping him get where he wanted to be.

Sometime later I made a huge bird from
the weekend section of the *Star* and a bowl of
paste. He was reading the *Star Weekly* when
he died, he left the story unfinished. I don't
know which story. I suppose I could find it on
microfilm; it's something I've thought about

doing, through the years, and never got to. But I made a newspaper bird and put it in the fireplace. The coloured ink flamed out in gold and green, brilliant purple. Then I went and watched the smoke from the chimney thin out and join the stars.

My mother outlived him by almost thirty years, but in her last months I could feel him on the move. They'd sent a message to him, at his cabin out in the hinterland of the afterlife, and he packed up an extra shirt and his harmonica and started the long trek into town. Nights when I stayed over in her apartment, on the pullout sofa in the living room, listening to her troubled coughing, I could see him sitting beside a little campfire, his bedroll laid out under the moon. One sleepless night I went onto her balcony to look at the northern lights, a fantastic dancing display, heaven astir. I was getting ready to hand her over. I'd never felt closer to him.

He blew into town around Christmastime, found himself a room in a boarding house, and settled down to wait. I dreamed about him

every night. He wandered around the streets,
got himself a haircut, played his harmonica in
the evenings in the neighbourhood bar. Down
below we did her a final Christmas. I think she
had set herself that goal, and a week later she
packed it in.

When she arrived at the heavenly city,
although she was occasionally a thorny com-
panion, I think he greeted her with incredible
joy. While the rest of us were making phone
calls, contacting relatives, ordering flowers,
he showed her the celestial sights, the angel-
wings, the pillars, the harps, before they began
the long journey back to his homestead. Both
their bad hearts blissfully irrelevant. They
could walk forever.

So now I'm the grownup, the owner of land,
the grower of corn for myself and the raccoons.
I sit in the dirt, turning out the last of the weeds.
The blade of my trowel disturbs a cricket. He
runs in a panic up over my bare knee, and that
scares him even more. Hey, cricket, I mean
you no harm.

D minor

In order for metaphor to work, one of its
halves has to be familiar. *The frizzool thrums
with excorpiance.* Whose mental life is en-
riched by this? The handful of people in the
world who are conversant with *frizzool* can
exclaim at the aptness of *excorpiance.* And
vice versa. But what if the audience at large
is familiar with neither? (As in this case:
I made the whole thing up. *I* don't even know
what I'm talking about, so what hope is there
for you?)

I've discovered a perfect metaphor that is,
alas, for reasons you'll soon understand,
inaccessible to a wide readership. Notice I say
"discovered." True metaphors aren't invented;
they lie around in the given world, like toilet
floats and acorns, until someone thinks to
notice their communality.

Bear with me, while I see if I can make this
work for you.

I'll begin with the staircase landing. It's in an old frame dormitory building at a music camp in the Laurentians. Worn linoleum covers wooden floors. Barefoot walking sounds wonderful; a distillate of all that's good about the family cottage. (*Pad, pad, pad, Timothy Tiger pads through the jungle.*)

The stairway goes up from the outside door. (Did I mention the wide verandah, overlooking the lake?) At the landing, two short sets of steps continue up, left and right, to the hallway on the second floor. Here's what happens: you're walking along this upper corridor to get from your room to the other outside door at the end. When you come to the landing, you have to descend the one set of steps, cross it, and then climb the other set to continue along the hall. Down, one footfall on the landing, and up the other side. You find yourself doing this all the time, and you quickly learn to lean into it, reach out your bare foot, and avoid the landing altogether. Bottom step . . . to bottom step. It makes a little hiatus in the sound

pattern of your footsteps that you're alert
to if you've been playing chamber music all
morning, listening for syncopation, hemiola,
the vagaries of rhythm. You let your body fall
forward, momentum carries you across, and
you climb on up the other side.

As you rush in and out to change into your
bathing suit, or get your glasses, or retrieve the
music you forgot for the Haydn trio, this little
holding back and then free-fall of your body
becomes one of the small casual private plea-
sures that adds buoyancy to your already
buoyant day.

And now the minor scales. The gap that
characterizes the melancholy sound of the
upper part of a minor scale is indicated on the
page by an accidental. A sharp or a flat, sometimes a natural, a fluttering flag warning of the
raised 7th. In the incessant practising of piano
technique, fingers dropping onto keys, ham-
mers hitting strings, this gap is a portal, an
invitation to rise above mechanics. The major
scales are righteous, chock-a-block, they frolic

up and down the piano like kittens tumbling on a carpet. The minor scales rise and fall through the same landscape with no less confidence. But they're intimate with the textures of shadow.

The D minor scale is the scale the piano was born to play. B flat to C sharp. From the upper black note of the group of three, across the landing, to the lower black note in the group of two. The fingers fall naturally over the configuration of notes. *Oh yes, yes.* How I wish I could show you, play it for you! But we're here on our separate pages, mine miles away from yours. You're going to have to take my words for it.

Of course you can see where I'm headed. The carpenter and the piano maker went about their business to build a flat geometry: stairs, a keyboard. And then I put them to use: footfall, fingers. Each spanning a chamber for the habitation of spirit. It's not simile. It's not a question of "like" or "as." They *are* the same thing, giving rise to the same small thundering of joy.

Essential services

Writers do our breathing for us, when life becomes so difficult that we can't do it for ourselves. When we're scared of airplanes and have to get to Vancouver, when we want sex and there's nobody viable around, when we're too full of excitement to turn our hands to anything, we go and find a book. A poet speaks to us of loss, and we know we're not alone.

When that Belgian ferry went down a few years ago, the newspapers described a local hero. They called him the "human gangplank." He hooked his feet over the rail of the sinking boat, stretched out, grasped a pier, a lifeboat, something that was stable or afloat, and let other passengers walk across his back to safety. Ten people, eleven, I'm not sure of the actual count. Then, and this to me is the incredible part of the story, when he knew he'd had enough, he unhooked his feet and scrambled forward into the rest of his life. He was a hero, not a martyr.

Where do writers go in winter? When they need to come in out of the cold, who do they turn to? Even poets need clean underwear.

I wish for them a perpetual garden adjacent to their back doors. Peas in the pod, red currants, cabbages. And for each of them a sensible cat, who understands when to frisk and when to gather into a pool of silence. A cat who will climb onto their shoulders and murmur in their ears: *It's time; get up now; go on.*

File folders

Manila file folders. During my childhood they were everywhere: in my father's study, my mother's desk drawers, in boxes in the basement beside the canned peaches. Used, folded inside out and turned around, used again. I liked them as objects, for the system they represented. Alphabetization, order. I used to wonder if they were designed to fit file cabinet drawers, or if the drawers were built to fit them. Or if the compatibility was just a happy accident.

The contents, on the other hand, like books with no pictures, belonged to the adult world. It's only now, in retrospect, that I've learned to read the files as history, as a record of the complicated texture of family. My mother's files contained financial accounts, minutes of committee meetings, letters. Notification, from 1931, of her acceptance to do an M.A. at Columbia, which she couldn't pursue because she didn't have the sixty dollars for tuition,

never mind that she'd fallen in love with a
Canadian and had to move north. The bulk of
my father's were related to the church: rough
drafts of Sunday School manuals that he
wrote to earn some extra money, papers from
the Engineering Department of the City of
Vancouver that authorized him to operate the
church's archaic furnace, records of weddings
and burials. Sermons: "The Cross," "Judas
Was Also a Son of God," his Mother's Day
blockbuster "Mothering or Smothering." He
had one wooden butterbox, itself miraculously
the right size for file folders, that he reserved
for "keewah," garbage too funny for the
wastebasket. He told me that "keewah" meant
"buffalo shit," in what language he never speci-
fied. Maybe it's a word he invented.

Now these files are all in cartons in my
second bedroom. The lives of my parents,
reduced, stacked against the wall. From time
to time, when I feel up to it, I dip into them.
Sometimes it's safe enough. The Christmas
card list. Car expenses for the trip back to

Ontario, July, 1949. But there's always the danger of blistering honesty. Diaries, letters, details of biography that pierce my heart.

She almost left him, once, and stayed because she found herself pregnant with me. I sit in my house, on the floor of the second bedroom. It's one of those rare midwinter afternoons when the Ontario skies have taken on a deep Alberta blue; the packet of letters beside me spills open into a shaft of sunlight. I am neither here nor there, then nor now. By a whisker, by a whisper, in a winter of discontent, I might not have existed at all. But listen, I know the story: I crossed the Rockies from Vancouver to Calgary tucked into a laundry basket, sound asleep. My tiny heartbeats fluttering in my fontanel. I spent the next six years nourished and treasured beneath that Calgary sky. Now here is the shadow to put beside that blue. The melancholy wisdom of the minor scale.

GIRL'S BEST FRIEND

Walk, walk, my morning walk around the block.
I almost didn't come out. Woke up from yet another springtime music camp nightmare feeling
fuzzy, and sorry for myself, so I sat in bed with a
cup of coffee and knit a few rounds on a sock.
I concentrated on keeping my two little fingers
relaxed. I hadn't realized they were tense until
last week, when they started to play hell with
the violin. My mother was a tense knitter, and
I learned it all at her knee, in the time-honoured
fashion. Casting on, casting off, knit, purl, and,
unfortunately, her grim-as-death attitude.
I thought I'd overcome it, the rest of my fingers
look loose enough, I can comfortably sail
through a sock now in jig time. But there they
were again this morning, my little fingers, down
at the bottoms of my hands where I couldn't
see them while I knit, rigid as chopsticks.

After half a dozen rounds I got out of bed.
I know these walks are a good thing. So out

I came, and settled into the rhythm of foot
to sidewalk.

I'm trying to kill two birds with one stone.
I've set each of my writing classes a different
topic this week, and for my own contribution
I want to write a piece that consolidates the two.
A practice that was frowned on in university;
it was dangerous to slide copies of the same
essay under the doors of two profs at once.

But university is long gone. Now I can walk,
write, knit, play the violin, if I'm a functioning
grownup I can do what I like, can't I? I'm invent-
ing my own life, I can ignore the wailing back-
wash of nightmare and screaming little fingers.

I turn the first corner, looking at the front
gardens, one after another. Neighbourhood
flower beds have been characterized, this past
week, by the deployment of the grape hyacinth.
Pulsing purple, in bunches, in lines, around
trees, along fences, and then, ignoring the
design of their shepherds, escaping through the
fences and heading off into the grass. I've called
it hyacinth week, I've taken a different route
every morning just to see what they'll think

of next. But now the blossoms are on the turn. My own have had it, I've snipped off the heads. The beds are taking a breather from that first springtime flourish, they're muscling up to settle into the long haul of summer.

I let my arms swing loosely, adjust my left shoulder, which should be level to take the violin, try to get the feel of how it should be when I play. The violin is directing my course these days, fertilizing the rich bed of metaphor that nourishes the rest of my life.

A journey or *A short fragment of a journey*, that's one of the topics. This walk around the block will take care of that. I'll stop in to get a paper, I've got a loonie in my pocket.

And the other topic: *What I first heard on awakening* or *What I wish I'd first heard on awakening.* The nightmare. I didn't hear it, exactly, but it filled the space, the first silence of my waking mind. It's strange that the anticipation of music camp, which I love, always engenders a lurid bouquet of dreams. The director of dreamland chose to revive both my parents for this one. I'm accustomed to nocturnal encounters with my mother, but I seldom meet my dad. It was nice to see him again, after all these years, up and moving, although it was brief. In the dream I lost him, lost them both. They'd driven me to the music camp, I was still a child, sitting in the back seat with my violin, the dates were wrong, we arrived two weeks early, they wandered off to find the camp director and never came back. Worn out with years of trying to figure them out, to pin them down, I took the easy way out and woke up. Spare me, I said to the dream director. We've been down this road before. Can't you come up with something new? Who are your writers?

My feet turn the second corner and I go back to my dad. My childhood. I remember the cracking of birch logs in the iron stove. I'm seven years old, just waking up in my sleeping bag. We're in a cabin in the woods on the southern edge of the Fraser Peninsula. I know it's birch from the way it spits and cracks, and from the tang in the smoke. He's downstairs getting ready to make breakfast. I hear him humming. A hymn, one of the Methodist tunes of his own childhood. No sound from my mom or brother; for both of them a vacation means sleeping in. They have to be prodded and coaxed, enticed; they roll out of sleep like large zoo animals coming out of the mud. For me and my dad it's up and at 'em.

At first the smell is singular, the burning birch. Then it's joined by coffee and bacon. Each of these has its attendant sound. The cottage has an aluminum percolator that plops and burbles.

These noises and smells, rich and various, are part of his plan; he's aiming them directly at my mother and brother. His humming breaks into song. Not the hymn; he's switched to a corny old country song from who knows where.

> *The only girl I ever knew*
> *Had a face like a horse and buggy*
> *Leaning on the lakeside*
> *Oh fireman save my child.*

As I shuck into my jeans and sweatshirt, ducking to avoid the slope of the plywood ceiling, I join in at the top of my lungs.

The fireman up the ladder went
The child was bigger than the fireman
Mother's teeth will soon fit in
Hang out the ice to dry.

I meet my dad in the stairwell at the final
verse.

Peeping through the knothole in Father's
    wooden leg
Who will wind my watch when I am gone,
    when I am gone?
Run get the axe there's a fly on baby's head
A boy's best friend is his mother.

My brother groans, and my mom says,
"Alright, al*right*, I'm awake!" On the stairs, we
grin. Got them both. Down to pancakes and
bacon.
    I discover myself smiling, singing full blast
as I round the last corner onto Cathcart.
"A boy's best friend is his mother." So I nip into
the variety, buy the paper, and head for home.

Grammar

*(and the overuse of the adjective, culturehood,
and Mrs. Tiggy-Winky Malaprop, our friend)*

I phone one of my writing students. Her
voice message says, "We are presently not here
at the moment." My first instinct is to shoot
myself. But ultimately I think it's sweet. I think
little grammatical weirdnesses are all sweet.

Take this baby. Let's not get into the theolog-
ical debate about original sin, or the tabula rasa.
Just take this baby; sweet fresh generic baby.
Old Noam says its grammatical furniture
is in there while it's still lying on its back, gur-
gling, looking out the upper half of the window
into the humming sky. Alien still to the verti-
cal; all four appendages slip equally easily
into its mouth. The baby doesn't know that
two of them will become the bottom, what
it stands on, connecting it to the earth, with all
that implies about hot coals, bunions, tap shoes,
fungal infections. Or that the other two will

point to the sky. This one particular baby,
fourth from the left with the kiss curl and the
wee furrowed brow, at the age of thirty-two
will dream that while her hands are flung
up to the heavens her fertile armpits grow a
daily crop of string beans. Which are harvested
by small earnest young men into wide wicker
baskets.

(It's appropriate and interesting to wonder
if this bean-grower is indeed the crabapple girl.
What gives it away? The produce perhaps, and
the flinging of arms.)

Notice Noam doesn't say the kid's *born*
with the grammatical furniture. Just that about
the time its mother introduces mashed carrot
the furniture is miraculously there, a battery of
empty plastic slide carousels. Ready and waiting
for name to glue itself to image and go into
the slot.

There's always the question, with mashed
carrot or orange juice: how will they affect
the stool, and consequently, the little bare bum?
Watch out for that dusting powder, it can

go straight to the lungs and terminate this
experiment when it's barely begun.

And who knows, about the mind of a baby?
Whatever's in there can sideslip and collide,
SURPRISE, the baby blinks and chuckles.

But this grip of language, this template, this
diagram of walking trails, a kilometre to the
inch, *keep back from the crumbling cliff edge,*
stays with us, resides in us. No, that's still not
right. It's not an attribute, it's part of what is. So
that a person, hearing the vague harmonies of
what's expected, might take aim and say,

> *she just let her children run rancid,*
> *you're an old hat at it,*
> *he uses her to sire his seed,*
> *I could see the light at the end of the*
>   *rainbow,*
> *they put him in solidarity confinement,*
> *there's that fallow period when people get*
>   *married and have babies,*
> *we looked at everything through a fine-*
>   *toothed comb,*

I emulated myself after Mark,
she was dressed to the nine irons,
I wasn't overly endowed with that movie.

And these vague miscalculations, these near misses, are also sweet. They spring from people's mouths and I'm all ears, I joyfully collect them and murmur (under my breath), *Thank you, oh thank you.*

While someone else, suddenly overcome with the gravity of what he finds himself doing (he's been minding his own business, rushing the dog through the park, there's a CBC radio van parked behind the cenotaph and with no time to prepare, to think, he's barely awake, he's only been hoping that the dog will shit quickly so he can grab a shower and catch the 7:30, there's a microphone in his face, he's been fingered as a Man on the Street), will burble out a word like "culturehood." And all across this great country of ours alert matrons pause suddenly over the cornflakes and think, "Culturehood! What the hell?"

And then there's the old adjectival stomp.
Swing yer partners.

> She slipped her striped pink satin blouse over
> her curly brown damp hair and looked out
> the dirty rain-streaked casement window at the
> deserted narrow windswept lane. She remem-
> bered the last careless lingering embrace as if it
> were yesterday. How he had held her in his
> rough comforting freckled arms, and . . .

Allemande left, if you're not yet lurching like
to puke. Which was it, striped or pink? Were the
stripes themselves pink? What was the other
colour? And just who is looking at these arms?
Maybe they could be rough *and* comforting. It's
a bit of a stretch, although a generous-spirited
reader might take that in, but why does it occur
to the heroine, in this context, that they're
freckled? Does she have eyes in the back of her
head? Can an embrace be both lingering and
careless? (*Exercise No. 1:* Invent the scenario in
which this makes sense.)

Old William Carlos said so much depends upon the red wheelbarrow. Yes, oh yes, William, Carlos, a name to die for, so much. A *red* wheelbarrow. Simply that. But the spectre of Miss Mayhew (gaunt, acidic, disapproving), Barton PS No. 1, rides the night, looming in the cluttered mind's attic: *Write a descriptive paragraph, using at least twenty adjectives. Make the reader see what you are seeing. Be evocative!*

(Maybe the stripes were red, and the background was white, so the overall effect was pink. Maybe he was hugging her from behind, and she looked down and saw his freckled arms circling her rib cage.)

Hurricane

Here's a riddle my dad used to ask:
Why did Adam call a cow a cow?
Because it looked like a cow.

Who gets to name the hurricanes? And
how do they manage to agree, worldwide, when
there's so much international disagreement
about almost everything else? We'll kill you for
your oil, or your water, or your religious per-
suasion, but Hey! You want to call that big
wind Susie? Go right ahead.

Hurricanes all used to be women, but
affirmative action has seen to that. Your house
may be blown to smithereens, but you can take
comfort in gender equity. Surely a corollary
to one of the fundamental feminist truths, that
it's okay for women to be competent, is that
it's okay for men to screw up. Surely we should
all be free to have good and bad days. There's
bad-day Mozart. There's a turn of phrase in one
of the horn concertos that sounds as if his

housekeeper had penned it (quilled it) one morning when she came in with the tea tray. Every time I hear it I think, "What the . . . ?"

We moved to Toronto when I was ten, to a street named Hendon. Fresh from British Columbia, with its in-your-face geography, I felt lost. I looked up Hendon at the library, in an effort to locate myself. The encyclopedia said it was an airfield in England where, at a postwar demonstration of aviation for civilians, several paratroopers plopped to their deaths in front of the grandstand because their chutes failed to open. Oh great, I thought, I'm sure glad I looked that up. The back half of the property, on Hendon, was a meadow full of wildlife. One morning, over breakfast, we counted twenty-seven pheasants. Now the property's covered with back-level splits and landscaped shrubbery, on a street called Tiger Lily Lane. Turn your back on your past for a few years and look what happens.

I used to wonder if a rose by any other name would smell as sweet. I'd go into my mother's

garden (on Hendon) and look at the blooms,
call them things like "cesspool" and "bile."
"Raw sewage" was a particularly lovely yellow
rambler. Then I'd smell them, to see if my
perception of the aroma was tinctured by the
connotations of the name. It's hard, sorting out
these sense perceptions, keeping them clean
of expectation. If you take a first swallow
from your mug of consommé while under
the impression that it's clear tea, the taste is
bound to be a blend of the two.

A recent e-mail from a friend described
the effect of Hurricane Floyd on New York City.
The only trouble they had was in Bay Head. He
said, "Now if I lived in a place called Bay Head
I think I would leave town when flooding was
starting. Just an idea." That got me thinking
about word games. *Invent localities whose names
ought to tell you something:* Fault-line Motel,
Tar-sands Dry Cleaning, Freeway Bird
Sanctuary.

Ah, you say, mere wordplay. But isn't that
what it's all about? The idea, the image, on the

one hand and our arsenal of vocabulary on the
other. And a ground, a bed of expectations.
The floor plan of the human mind.

My dad, the riddler, grew up in a farming
household, where once a year the clock-mender
came by to clean their clocks. (More word-game
material: stumbling unexpectedly on the literal
circumstance of a cliché.) One year, when the
guy had the pieces of the grandfather clock
spread out on the kitchen table, my dad added
a little flywheel he'd been carrying around
in his pocket. The guy was there for days,
assembling and reassembling, trying to make it
all fit. That extra flywheel didn't belong, any
more than Inuit throat-singing belongs in
Dickens, but he was fooled by the visual. My
dad tried the same stunt on me years later with
a jigsaw puzzle, but I spotted the extra piece
right away; the quality of the colour was
wrong.

Naming, naming. That *first fine careless
rapture*. Careless is wrong for the lingering embrace, but for rapture it's perfect.

Intermezzo

May these words be the music
may they enter the mind gently
a naked body entering silky water on a
                                    soft morning

may these words

may they

   part the mist
be liquid as otter, buoyant
above the speckled deep of turtle
open up
to the slow thumping breasted arc of heron

may these words be.

Sunlight takes the mist on its tongue
swallows
wipes the last blood-sweet stain
from its mouth
sets the cloth aside

the day goes about its morning business
horizontals are rolled up
blue water chops and glints.

Only the dragonfly registers a vestigial ache
remembers
the welcoming still perch of bare knee
bent over gunwale
searches with its wings for that small
                              sudden sweetness
of tender, word-thickened air.

Join the club

A friend came over to look at my garden.
I said, "I've got too much oregano."
"Yeah," she said, "who doesn't?"

J-words

Exercise No. 2: Make a list of words that begin with the initial of your name, and then do something with them.

Jane, Janet and Jethro. When they got older they sometimes speculated on their mother's evident fixation with the letter *J*. Were their names pious, if indirect, allusions to Jesus? Or did they reflect the restless energy of her hopes for them? Was her imagination caught by the cheerful recklessness of jalopy, jiu-jitsu, jazz? Did she see her children, down the long avenue of the future, always on the move? Jittery? Jumpy?

As children, though, their names were only an embarrassment, an annoyance. They could find plenty of words to describe the physical bullying: jarring, jabbing, jouncing. Jolting. But there were also tormentors with verbal skills. In locker rooms, Jethro's name coupled inevitably

with jacking off. Janet got Jolly Janet, from
teachers, until she swore never to smile
again. The French teacher experimented with
jeune Jane, but it was lame, and it never took
hold. Everybody knew the French teacher
was himself a jerk.

Middle age found Jethro, jackhammer in
hand, jaded on a job site; Janet teaching English
in Japan; Jane a botanist: juniper, jonquil,
jacaranda.

They each jumped into a jet to reconvene
for their mother's funeral. Standing on the jetty
at the family cottage, they watched their father
struggle with the lid on the jar of ashes, and
scoured their minds for appropriate words.

Jane whispered "journey." Jethro flung out
his arms and drew his sisters close to him.
The wind lifted the grey powder, sifted it into
the sky, where it thinned and disappeared.

Janet said, "Jeepers creepers."

KITCHEN SINK

"What's going on? She's got everything in
here but the . . ."

Are you getting restless? Is that last *J*
entry just too much for you? She's not paying
attention, you say, she's writing with one hand
tied behind her back, she's watching TV, she's
chewing gum. A patent exercise.

And you're right, it reads like bad-day
Mozart. You've found me out. Let me try to
make you care. I care, at that one point on the
dock, when the dad fumbles the urn's lid. It's
October, his wife's dead, and here he is at the
cottage with these three adult strangers. Since
they've grown he's thought of them as his
wife's children, not his own. She was the one
who'd talk to them on the phone, and tell him
their news as if they were characters in a book
she'd been reading. He once taught three small
children how to swim, in this very lake. A boy
and two girls. What has that to do now with

these black shoes they're wearing, that click
strangely on the wooden planking? His heart
is breaking, as he gives up the last vestige of his
wife to the wind, and they won't stop playing
their silly word game, even for this.

Jethro has calluses on his palms from the
handle of the jackhammer. No one knows
this but himself.

Perhaps elsewhere I've intrigued you, even
enchanted you; perhaps I've made you laugh.
Well, it's not always like that. Sometimes
there's only bread, with no butter. The sun
doesn't always go down in a blaze of glory.
Occasionally night simply falls, and nobody
notices. Horses go off their feed. Street lamps
burn out. Small gusts of wind blow dust
across an empty playground.

Last things

The other day I watched some television while
I ate my lunch. It was an old black-and-white
performance of *The Art of the Fugue,* played by
members of the Toronto Symphony. I spotted
several players I knew when I was a subscriber
to the TSO in high school. Already this had
put me in a melancholy reminiscent mood,
when the music came quietly to a halt. Letter-
ing scrolling up the screen, in the silence, said,
"Those were the last bars that Bach ever wrote."

.   .   .

James Thurber died in the two-hour pause
between pap smear and mammogram. Right
there in the City View Restaurant, my tears
spilled onto the page, onto the second half
of my sandwich, onto the table. Blind, irascible,
abusive, he'd been tended, during his last years,
by friends and a faithful wife on the strength
of how loving and amiable he used to be. In

the midst of my annual medical annoyances,
intrusive procedures, I ate the sandwich,
read the last pages of the biography, watched
him die, and cried. Even as a little child, looking
at his cartoons, I recognized his narrative
state of mind in my own head.

When he actually died, in November of
1961, I was in my first year of university. This
restaurant was a student hangout then. So I
hung out, wondering when the Good Life was
going to begin. But what was I doing when he
sadly breathed his last? Riding my bike,
reading Spinoza, figuring out where to buy
toothpaste. How could I have missed it?

.   .   .

We'd been at the cottage for two weeks when
my sister-in-law came up, with the news from
home that our cat had been killed. We thought
about how he had loved tobogganing. The kids
cried. Our car, parked under a tree by the lake,
still bore his dusty footprints on the hood.

.   .   .

My mother coughed during the slow movement of the string quartet, worried that she was
disturbing people.

"Go ahead and cough," I said. "Let it out."

A couple of weeks later she died. In the
spring I heard her cough again, on the CBC
broadcast of the concert.

MACAROON

Slipping into Tim's, dashing into Tim's. Into
Tim's, anyway, for a coffee, and there's a woman
in the parking lot bending over watching a
mechanic change her flat rear tire. Gravity's got
her, pulling down her long scarf, her coattails,
strands of hair, her dangling purse. If its force
were any stronger she'd collapse right into
the pavement.

 The mechanic's bent too, but it looks more
appropriate on him. Born to bend. She's all
falling question marks of apology. As if it's her
fault her tire's flat. The amber light on the cab
of his pickup, rotating, warning all the sailors:
Here's a silly woman with a flat. Beware.
Stay well out in the channel.

 Just ahead of the front wheel on the dark
tarmac, all perky insouciance, is a snow-white
macaroon.

 Oh, to have been here earlier! What was
the sequence? Did the woman drop it out the

window in surprise when the car first began
to hump and thud? Is it perhaps the mechanic's
macaroon? Was it part of a batch? Did one of
its mates conceal a cement nail, dropped into
the batter by a carpenter putting up shelving in
the bakery, that caused the flat?

When I come out with my coffee the
woman is gone, her car is gone, the mechanic,
his pickup and his flashing light are gone, but
the macaroon is still there. A powder puff, a
kiss; I don't have time for more metaphor
nor to wait and watch until somebody drives
over it, to see if it flattens onto the parking lot
or wraps itself onto the tire tread like a limpet
and takes off for the ride.

.   .   .

When I first got my computer I spent a week
playing with the voices. There's Ralph and
the Princess, Cello, Zarvox, Bubbles, Trinoids,
Deranged; nineteen of them altogether.
And what a time they must have in there
at night.

Princess: Has anyone seen my boa?

Zarvox: You and your damn boa! We'll miss
   the late movie if you don't hurry up,
   and I left the bike running.

Bubbles: Boa, boable, abble abble abble
   Bike running rubbling, bling, bling.

Zarvox: Christ! I don't know how we survive
   in this madhouse!

Deranged: It's meat and potatoes to some of
   us. Heeheeheeheeheehee.

My favourite is Fred. He's tired, laconic,
world-weary, he's been on the job for just too
long. His voice has a dying fall at the end of
every sound bite, like Eeyore, or Marvin the
Paranoid Android. I write him a domestic
poem, to see if I can surprise him out of his
profound dolour.

   washing machine
   dryer
   frigidaire
   ricer

dicer
slotted spoon
blender
broiler
double boiler
watch me make a macaroon

In order to get him to pronounce correctly
I have to fool around with spelling and spacing:

washing. machine . . . . .
dryer . . .
frih-jih-dare . . .
rice-er . . .
dice-er . . .
slot-ed spoon . . . . .
blend-er . . .
broil-er . . .
duh-bel . . boil-er . . .
wawch . . mi . . mayk . . a . . ma . . ca . . roon

Then click on Voices, click on Fred, click on
Read All, and away he goes. Ah, housework!

Ah, kitchen appliances! What an intolerable drag life is! But I get him with the last line; his voice quickens, he's interested despite himself: *Watch me make a macaroon!*

A person might ask, "Who *cares* if the macaroon stuck to the tire or to the pavement?" Let me tell you something: I do.

MALLARD DREAM

She glanced in the bathroom mirror and saw
that something peculiar was going on with
her hair. It had become enlarged, and by lifting
the front curls she could look into a chamber
where two ducks, a pair of mallards, were standing on her head. They were feeding contentedly
on flakes of dandruff, flakes as large and crisp
as potato chips. They crunched when the ducks
snapped them up in their bills. The part of her
hair forming the roof of this chamber let in
bars of soft light, so the whole set-up looked
like a swampy forest glade. She thought about
running for her camera, and the absurd
logistics of this woke her up.

She hadn't experienced any dandruff for
twenty years, but you can be sure that from
then on she was on the lookout for it.

She'd had her share of personal bodily
dreams, over the years. Chickens jumping on
her stomach, her feet rotting in an attempt

to meld with her roller skates; peeing into a disused metal feed hopper in the back shed of a Presbyterian parsonage. In that one she actually wet the bed, and not so long ago that she chose, under normal circumstances, to talk about it.

But this dream, the mallards feeding off her production of outsize scales of dandruff, joined another dream, the bean dream, which until now had been in a category all by itself. In the bean dream she was lying on her back in a nest of cosy comforters. The room was built of bamboo, the soft slatted sunlight was the same kind of light that fell in stripes over the feathered backs of the ducks. The comforters were arranged in a corner on a hard-packed dirt floor. Primitive, but she was being treated like a treasure. Like the goose who laid the golden eggs. Obsequious people came to feed her, fan her, cater to her every need.

And every evening, it must have been at sunset because the light had changed from a soft yellow to a rosy glow (the dream was big on cliché), two small men with large flat

baskets came for the harvest. She was growing
string beans of incredible luxuriance in her
armpits. They grew in bunches, long and thick.
The men knelt quietly, one on each side of her;
she raised her arms above her head so they
could pick them. There was no pain involved.
The beans made a pleasant popping sound
when they came away from the stems. There
were enough to fill the baskets, and by the
next evening she had grown more. Early in the
morning, she heard the men leave on their
bicycles for the market. They were apparently
making a killing.

Although the circumstances were pleasant,
the nest was comfortable, the food good, the
people friendly, she knew she was confined
there. She had no present wish to leave, but
she knew that should she at some point
become bored and want to move to some less
peculiar ambiance, she would be restrained.
In the way that the impulse to photograph the
ducks snapped her out of that sylvan scene,
an attempt to escape here would bring an end

to her captors' good will. As it was, she drifted happily on to blank sleep.

What would the next dream be? Her belly button had been sewed shut, early on, as part of the closure from a hernia operation. Otherwise, what a wealth of exotic glittering fishes might have flourished there. Lint transformed into talking tetra, running sixteenth-notes, rattling crabapples.

Negative space

The curved oak leaf darting across the smooth snow-covered road in the early-morning dark is not a mouse.

And when the outer door opens and the plastic bag of advertising hung on the handle swings into the gap, it's not the large sloppy-tongued dog shouldering in to gulp down his breakfast.

.   .   .

Exercise No. 3: Read the first paragraph of *A Tale of Two Cities*. Using only that information, write a list of things you would *not* expect to find in the book.

a Valley girl
a cross-dresser
open-heart surgery
a dinosaur
papaya juice
a Rolodex

windsurfing
a Wal-Mart
anyone with AIDS
a polyester pantsuit
a pogo stick
Dutch elm disease
nude swimming
an electric violin
a split infinitive
a bingo dauber
Inuit throat-singing
a flapper
a hangnail

.   .   .

This morning the parking lot beside the library
was empty. It was seven o'clock, it had only
been light for half an hour. Even the coffee
shop was still closed. A full moon was setting
behind the church spire, insubstantial in the
lightening sky. I looked at the completely
unremarkable parking lot, thought ahead three
hours to the bustle of the fall plant exchange.

How would it differ from the way I was imagining it? Nothing ever pans out the way you expect it to.

When my father died, and I flew home from Saskatoon, fresh baby sitting on my lap, nothing would do for my mother but that we should have a bouquet of roses and baby's breath beside his picture, on a table in the church narthex.

This became my task. No florist had baby's breath. I had brought along a breathing baby, but it wouldn't do; we were flummoxed by alternate meanings.

"Surely," my mother said, "somebody in the congregation must have some in their garden." She gave me the church membership list.

Hello. You don't know me, but I'm ——'s daughter. He died yesterday. My mother wonders if you have any baby's breath in your garden.

I made only one of these absurd calls. Then I came to my senses, put my foot down firmly on my mother's wishes, and insisted on fern fronds.

Thirty-two years ago this week. And this
morning a woman brought baby's breath to the
plant exchange. As I'd predicted, here was the
unpredictable.

Now it's planted in my garden, tucked in
between a clump of daisies and the coreopsis.
So the next time he dies, I'll simply go to
the garden with my scissors. *Here, Mother,
here's plenty.*

Out of nothing

First night at the writing class. Empty room, scuffed linoleum floor, aluminum tables and chairs. Cement-block walls, painted an institutional pale green. These walls always bring back a tired stack of childhood memories: church basement rummage sales, or interminable visits to ancient great-aunts in old folks' homes.

And then I watch the people come in. Strangers, filling up the chairs. All of them wrapped in their "stranger" cloaks like unopened presents, shoulders held in tight.

The first tentative filament of the word game. A slow thin daisy chain, one person to the next: aardvark, zoo, panda, teddy bear, lullaby, bough breaks, earthquake . . .

Second time around the circle, another strand: hot, cold, frigid, ice man, tongs, toothpick, cavity, dentist, plaque, flack, bombardier . . .

The shoulders loosen, they get used to the sounds of their own voices, they're interested

despite themselves, forget themselves, the
words take strength and begin to breathe.

Pumpkin, ghoul, goblin, monkey,
writhe, coil, tendril, growth, shoot, grapple,
climb, soar . . .

We have liftoff. Now we can sit back and
watch the images grow, clamber up the green
walls, float into the unused spaces of air,
hover just below the ceiling, buoyant, accumu-
lating, coalescing like rain into the splendid
radiance of story.

PENNY

I've always been superstitious about pennies.
Their spending power is plummeting at an
alarming rate, but I always pick them up
from the sidewalk or the floor of the car and
put them in my wallet. Show the money gods
you care and they'll shower you with riches.

"Don't put that penny in your mouth," my
mother said, "you don't know where it's been."

I always tried to find a way around my
mother's pronouncements. If we don't know
where it's been, why do we assume it's been
somewhere dirty?

"This one started in a laundry," I told her.
"And then went to a hospital. And then a
church." I was scrambling for every clean place
I could think of. "Then an old lady kept it in her
handkerchief drawer for seven years, and then
she gave it to her granddaughter, and *she* took it
into the bath with her every night and *scrubbed*
it with her brother's toothbrush. And her cat

liked the taste of soap, so he licked it clean
every night after the bath. And . . ."

My mother moved to laughter, at the web
I was spinning.

"Well, don't put it in your mouth anyway,"
she said. Captivated, but not convinced.

I suspected her concern was based more on
having seen a quarter go in one end of me and,
in the fullness of time, come out the other, but
I couldn't get her to admit it. I knew precisely
where that quarter had been and there was no
chance I'd be putting *it* in my mouth again.
I've still got it, tucked away in a little box
with an old IUD and a hank of hair. I thought
about it in university, when we were studying
Shakespeare: how a king can go a progress
through the guts of a beggar.

Where have these words been? They circulate,
like money, like notes. Schubert used D minor
for *Death and the Maiden* and then I take it
and slide it into metaphor. Words get warped
and battered, they suffocate, scream, and we pick
them up and use them over with nary a thought.

Today I got a penny change from Tim's,
was stashing it safely in my pocket, when I had
a sudden thought. "There are no money gods.
Grow up. Time to get a grip." I thought to
toss it in the garbage bin, but caught myself in
time. This is not about money. I cradled it in my
fingers, rubbed my thumb across the secret
Braille, detail of its journey.

QUAKER STATE

Stinking hot back seat, my shorts are itchy,
I've read all the comics. The old Chevy's
so packed with stuff I can't get my feet to the
floor, I have to stick them straight out, over the
brown suitcase and the duffel bag. The windows
are wide open, the prairie air is pouring in,
but it doesn't help. It's not a breeze. It's more
like hot marble pillars, pillows, cushions of
smothering air.

My brother's reading *Mad* magazine. I turn
sideways, stick my big toe under the edge and
flick it up out of his hands. His moods are an
unknown substance. Sometimes he would
think this was funny. Today he's furious. His
anger fills up the car, billows, buffets against the
heat. My mom reaches into the big thermos by
her feet, passes us each a dripping ice cube.

I look at her hand. Her domestic hand—
cooking, spanking, feeding clothes through
the wringer. Now it's hot and wet, holding the

glinting ice, far from home in the middle of Montana. We're all in the middle of Montana, for crying out loud, and my dad's the only one who's happy, the only one who seems to have faith that we'll get anywhere.

The ice disappears as soon as I wrap my mouth around it, I know it's hot water by the time it hits my stomach.

Does your husband misbehave,
Grunt and grumble,
Rant and rave?
Shoot the brute some Burma-Shave.

The signs flash past, a prairie poem, the lines a hundred yards apart. Prairie. Grass, dust, telephone poles.

My dad's whistling. Easy for him. He believes that if he puts his car on one end of a road it'll take him to the other end. He's done this before. I think the car is an ant. We'll never get out of here. We'll never get to anything.

My dad says, "What'll it be, Barnyard Cribbage or the alphabet?"

Barnyard Cribbage involves counting animals. It's competitive, played in teams. Right-
side passengers look right, left-side passenger
and the driver look left. First team to get to
fifty wins. The rules are very specific: no
one sighting can count for more than ten
points. A herd of forty cows, a flock of sheep,
only ten. And the rule to end all rules, end the
game: if you see a man sitting in a backhouse,
with the door open, pants down around his
knees, reading the coloured funnies, you win.
My brother actually achieved this once, when
we were stopped for gas in Idaho. He had to
sneak up through the woods to confirm the
coloured funnies. This took its rightful place
as one of the highlights of our family history.

Alphabet is communal, rather than competitive. You collect letters, in order, from road
signs and billboards. They have to be confirmed
by at least one other player. (This last codicil
was invented when I still couldn't tell *P* from
B.) Only one letter per sign.

This particular godforsaken chunk of
Montana has more road signs than animals,

although there are precious few of either, so
we choose Alphabet. Even my brother agrees,
although he prefers Barnyard Cribbage. He
must be feeling guilty about getting mad at me.
There's another set of *Burma-Shave* signs so
off we go, with one of the *A*'s.

By the time we reach *P* we're getting hungry.
We stop for lunch at a restaurant on the main
street of a small town.

Plain cheese sandwich and a strawberry
milkshake. That's what it always is, for me. No
lettuce, no mayonnaise. Although I'm always
too shy to state those specifications. My dad
has to do it.

"She wants," he says, with the right smile
to make the waitress amenable, "a slice of
bread, butter, a slice of cheese, butter, and the
other slice of bread. That's all. Nothing else."
The waitress walks away, shaking her head but
smiling. Such is my dad's gift.

I pray, too, my own silent prayer as the waitress leaves. *And please, please, don't bring it on a
warm plate. Have the plate as cold as possible.*

Don't have it in a warming oven, or fresh out
of the dishwater, or sitting in the sunlight. Have it
cold. Cold like a tile floor first thing in the morn-
ing. I never say this out loud, or make my
dad say it. I've never even told him I wish it.
I know when enough is enough.

  The sandwich arrives and I study it, plan how
to eat it: bite off the crusts, all the way around,
and then flatten the rest of it with my thumbs
and index fingers until the bread is like a paste,
welded to the cheese with the slippery butter.
Then I think I'm a Mexican, eating a tortilla.
(I know now this bears no relation to a tortilla,
but I didn't know it back then. The word *tortilla*
was so exactly right for the gummy little wad
in my hand that I never thought to wonder
whether it was accurate.)

  I walk out of the shade of the adobe hut. My
tight black pants hug my crotch. My sweat smells
of burro. I walk to the well, drink from the dipper.
Return to my burro, tethered in the shadow. Open
the saddlebag, take out two tortillas. I sit down in
the dirt, lean back against the adobe, and eat.

The reverie doesn't last. There's a ceiling fan, an MOR station on the radio, grime on the front windows that look out to the main street, the only street, of yet another steamy midwestern town. I'm a scratchy girl again. I climb into the back seat of the old Chevy, kick my brother, and look out the side window. There's a gas station across the street. I have to wait until the car's in motion. *Yes.* The impossible *Q*. Quaker State.

RAVE

"A compelling tour de force, based on the English alphabet, covering the emotional and mental territory of the entire world."
Move over, Sue Grafton.

Snapshot

Image on a square of paper, black and white,
fuzzy grey, pattern that focusses into memory.
"Look, there's . . ." Story takes over.

Neighbourhood babies on a blanket under
a tree. The mothers have all stepped aside, they
don't make it into the picture. Now they're all
long gone, and the babies themselves have
grown, learned walking and talking, gone
through primers and spellers, long pants and
puberty, church socials, gall-bladder operations,
menopause. Have fought in the war, made a
thousand casseroles and met, all six of them,
their various ends. Might as well pick up that
blanket by the corners, and deposit these
bouncing babies in the graveyard.

But back at the beginning they're still babies,
with a dapple of light and shadow on their six
downy heads. The dad who is taking the picture
will pick up his tripod and wander away, leaving
the babies to their mothers. The next picture

he takes is of his Model T. Great-uncle Harry,
smiling in his uniform, poses beside it. Two of
the mothers go into the house for plates of
sandwiches and the lemonade. The babies roll
off the blanket, face-first into the prickly
grass. Some of them chuckle, one of them cries.

There's a melancholy that clings to the picture like faded perfume. I watch as it animates
into the what-happened-next, I'm in thrall
to the illusory power of retrospect. I want it
back for them, the breeze in the tree, the
lemonade, the laughter. They had it there, at
that instant of the picture, but something went
wrong; they grew up, got old, and died.

What I really long for is a different world
altogether, a world without graves, where the
passage of time doesn't inevitably do us in.

"Tell us a story! Tell us a story!"

They all hop around, tugging at her. The Baby deftly clamps her suck-thumb blanket into her armpit in order to free one hand, which she then clamps wetly onto the hem of her mother's skirt. They pull her over to the sofa, importunate tugboats docking a cumbersome liner.

There are only three of them, although they're making enough racket for twenty. They still smell of bathwater. Their ears are damp.

She's the mother, it's all domestic, but she has trouble focussing on them. What she wants to be talking about is how the roof on the back extension of the house across the street looks as if it has socked itself onto the back of the house. She can hear the noise it must have made, like shooting a bolt. Icicle knives hang from the eaves.

They fly in, from the left, in tight formation.
A cutting-down dive at the peripheral vision just

above her left eyebrow. She can't tell what they
are; planes being driven, or captive creatures
being flown, she doesn't know. She does recognize
the pilots, though. They're those sinister bald
green-eyed creatures from the Frosst pharma-
ceutical calendars. Dingbats, from Dingbat
Land. They hung on the walls of all the doctors'
offices of her childhood.

That tight formation of eyes, blazing, aiming at
her, but above her head, so she can't look directly
at them. At the last possible breath-choking
minute they part, sweep past, and scream up out
of the dive; the hyena-laughter bubbles back to
surround her.

Can she help it if hanging icicles make her
think of the vulnerable fontanel? And fontanels
of the patella, that floating silver-dollar kneecap
that slithers around sickeningly under experi-
menting fingers?

The boy's kneecaps are squared off. He's wearing the pyjamas with the short pants. His legs
are primly crossed, he's looking at her seriously

like a little old man. Now that they've got her herded onto the sofa they're quiet, waiting.

The Baby, independent little creature that she is, has fixed herself a cave of cushions, is lying back in her sleepers, thumb in her mouth, the ragged blanket clutched up beside her face.

It's the other one, curiously, the eldest of the three, who cuddles in. Knees drawn up, she tucks her flannel nightgown around her toes, and slumps against her mother's arm. The weight of her is like a sack of potatoes.

"Do you see," the mother asks them, "how that roof over there looks like it was snapped onto the house by a giant Lego-builder?"

But they're not to be distracted. The boy glances politely out the window, registers the observation, and sighs.

"Do you want to hear about the little family whose brakes failed on a mountainous road in Mexico, and their Airstream trailer came *that close* to backing over a precipice?"

The boy says, "That's too scary." And then adds, "For The Baby."

"Ah."

They all call her The Baby. They probably always will.

"How about the snail I once saw doing a poo-poo at Spanish Banks?

The Baby's eyes light up. "Poo-poo," she says.

She's got the attention of one of them, anyway.

The Baby has to remove her thumb in order to speak, and the suction makes a little popping sound. P-wonk. It's a small punctuation mark that precedes her cryptic messages, like the musical jingle in VIA stations that alerts us to an announcement about incoming trains.

"How big was it?" the girl asks.

"How big was what?"

She says "the snail" and the boy says "the pew-pew," at the same time.

So she's caught them all, with a shitting snail. Rule No. 1 for a Raconteur: Know your audience.

"Well. We went there on the bus. We packed a little lunch, and made a day of it."

"Who's 'we'?" the girl asks.

"You and me. This happened about fifteen years from now. You were out in Vancouver going to school, and I went out to visit you. *You*," she says to the boy, "were old enough to stay by yourself for a whole week! You were driving the car, and everything."

He can't believe it. He tucks one foot up under himself.

"What kind of car?" he says, suspicious.

"Oh, I dunno. You'll have to wait and see. Heaven only knows where The Baby was by then." They all look at her, and she grins. *She* knows, but she's not telling.

The Dingbats began bombing when she was a small child. Or they'd land somewhere, sneak up and capture her, and take her to their cave to saw off her arms. Sometimes they'd hang her up on the cave wall with chains, and she'd get to watch them saw off somebody else's arms.

"We went to Spanish Banks on the bus. We rode and rode and rode . . ." (The Baby is beginning to droop, the three of them watch her heavy eyelids) " . . . and then we got off the bus and we walked and walked and walked and walked . . ." (Her eyelids clunk shut, her little mouth stops sucking, her thumb falls halfway out.)

The boy edges off the sofa, switches off the lamp over The Baby's head, tucks the tattered suck-thumb blanket around her and climbs gently back up beside her.

"Yeah?" he says. "Go on."

" . . . and walked, until we finally got there.

"We walked across the sand, and put our towels down between two big logs. The wood was bleached white, and worn away by the wind and the pounding sea. Millions of creatures lived in the dark wet cracks. Across the inlet we could see the houses climbing the mountainside into the silent forest. Big dark trees, like the Ents, blended into a carpet of deep green, think-ing at each other. Those trees knew each other so well they didn't need any words. They just sat there and thought, and all the other trees knew what they meant.

"We'd spent so much time riding and riding and riding and walking and walking and walking . . ."

"Yeah, we know," the boy says. "The Baby's asleep already."

"Oh, yeah. Sorry. What we were was tired and hungry. So we sat there in the sunshine and unpacked our lunch. The logs were warm from the sun, and we could hear the water lapping on the shore."

The Baby twitches, her mouth makes three or four silent sucking motions, and she sighs.

The Dingbats come at her in the daytime now, she doesn't need to be asleep. She guesses that's progress. They still scare her, but she can see them a little better.

She's fighting them with the Bach two-part Inventions. She's learned three in the last month, she intends to learn all fifteen. She goes at it slowly, steadily, figures out the fingering, writes it in, learns a couple of bars hands-separately, then puts them together, goes on to the next bar. The

Inventions are built like small solid redoubts,
four-square, logical. The two hands speak to each
other, working together, working against, helping
each other out; in the one she's just learned there's
a magical fleeting place where both thumbs hit
the same note. She could refinger it, let one hand
do the work, but she likes the feel of it, her two
thumbs briefly touching, talking without words
like the trees. It's only for an instant, it's a
sixteenth-note and it's going by at a hell of a
clip; the thumbs coincide and then raddle off to
tell their separate stories.

With each one she learns, she can feel the Ding-
bat bombing missions becoming slightly more
vicious. As if they're afraid they're going to lose.

"What was in the little lunch?" the girl asks.

"The lunch. Well, you were pretty clever.
You made the lunch because *I* was visiting *you*
in your very own apartment. You had crab
meat, and crackers, and a whole head of lettuce
that we split in half, and you'd *very* cleverly put
a couple of bottles of beer in a thermos."

"Beer?! Gak."

"So we ate the lunch, and drank the beer, and we were down to the apple cores when you saw a very small snail right beside your arm, on the log. It wasn't the kind of snail we have here in the garden, it was *much* smaller than that. Smaller than a pea, bigger than a pinhead. About the size of a grain of rice.

"It was moving around, so we knew it wasn't just an empty shell. It was tilted up on its side, and rocking a bit. It was so small it was really hard to see, and every time we leaned over to get a good look we bumped our heads together. So we finally got organized and moved the lunch stuff out of the way and lay down on our stomachs. It was tricky, because there wasn't much space and by that time you were bigger than I am."

"What?"

"Yep. You noticed something poking out of it, and it seemed to be getting bigger. At first we thought it might be having a baby, but neither of us knew if that's how snails *have* their babies.

"Then we figured it out. It was trying to have a poo. It was working and working, and then it would get tired and stop for a while, and then work and work some more. You thought it might want some help, so you got a stick about the size of a bobby pin and put it under the snail and it grabbed onto that stick with its foot and said, 'Oh thank you, thank you, big kind creature whoever you are,' and gave one final big heaving push and the piece of poop came right out on the stick."

The boy says, "It never said thank you, thank you."

"Not in so many words, no. It said it in snail-talk. That's just like Ent-talk, only smaller."

They sit on the sofa, in the twilight, listening to The Baby breathe. The roof across the street doesn't look to her like Lego any more, it's just a roof.

Up they go, the mother takes The Baby, the boy brings her blanket.

The girl says, "Couldn't it have been cream soda?"

"Nope. As I remember it, you were pretty fond of beer back then."

The boy says, "Did they get down safely?"

"Who?"

"The little family in Mexico."

"Oh, sure. They coasted backwards all the way down into Mexico City. Ask me about it tomorrow."

U-turn

We're getting to the end, picking our way
through the dark thicket of the final letters.
This is the alphabet's outback, letters that give
rise to prickly words of myth and science.

That little family in the trailer didn't have
room to turn, and had to back all the way to
the beginning. The mother of the other little
family, mother of the bedtime story, was teaching her children how to turn time inside out
and reminisce in reverse.

As a mere classification tool, the alphabet
has a short shelf life. People change their
names, get married, die or move, and directories
deteriorate. Even this book's plan is restless.
It seemed a simple matter at the outset,
an entry for each letter, but now there are two
each for *g, j* and *m,* and "Intermezzo" breaks
into song.

Why am I dawdling here, killing time,
when the journey's almost done? I feel a bite

in the October wind, there are storms in the
North Atlantic. It will be winter soon,
and the book will be finished. Then what will
we all do?

Voice

It's her voice that gets to me.

I feel the thin trembling chill, the bird-bone
vulnerability of naked shoulder blades, the sting
of sharp driveway gravel on little bare feet. Feet
that should be cosily tucked up in bunny slip-
pers, while she drinks her cocoa in the firelight
and hears the story of Piglet and Pooh. I see
the dark rain, the shouldering shapes of the
crabapple trees, I see the small white nape
of her neck glowing in the street lamp as she
bends her head forward, beyond tears.

But it's the voice that continues to curl at the
outside edge of my eyelid, flickers like a moth
trapped under a wiper blade, flutters to get
away but stays there, stuck, jammed, pleading.

It's the voice of a little child, in a state of
distress, a state of anguish, this is no cut finger
or abraded knee, not the scraps and scrapes of
childhood, but the kernel inside that voice,
the white worm of soul.

It's asking for help. Not in so many words,

there are no words, no specifics, just the jagged
cadence of fear, of bone-tired desperation. She's
too close to the crumbling verge of giving up.

The voice scales and slides, floats, gathers
itself, begins again, the same relentless story.
It's important. I'm weeding the iris bed, a
tedious exacting job, clipping back the faded
leaves, taking up pebbles and small fronds of
clover. I scrape away the microcosm of moss,
turning the earth with the merest tip of a
kitchen knife to leave the rhizomes undis-
turbed, ready for winter. I stop and sit back on
my muddy heels in the sunlight, listen to the
urgency in that plaintive wind-torn cry.

It's a song, sheeted-out, a flurry of notes,
tumbling, glass casements sliding to crash,
sliding, caught sideways in an up-lift of wind,
slicing the sky, cartwheeling back, crash.

I listen, and somewhere inside me (armpit,
heart, scalp), somewhere in there the voice has
found a fertile tissue, a scrap of resonance,
something of itself.

I ease the rounded knife tip under the rhizome,
open the cooling earth to the sunlight. Listen.

Word list

Exercise No. 4: Write a piece using all of the following words: clouds, Seattle, petroleum jelly, Vaseline, baby, crib, pins, needles, needle-point, embroidery, shirt, buttons, cushion, couch, chair.

"Well you know, Harvey's always got his head in the clouds. Most often as not his hand in his pants, too, I don't know how many times I've told him about it, but it's a habit now, hitting him doesn't work, I guess I'll have to get some handcuffs.

"And I don't think he heard anything he shouldn't have. Ethel and I were drinking coffee and I didn't know he was sitting under the table or I'd have made him go outside. He gets so sneaky and quiet sometimes.

"And anyway, what's a four-year-old know about big words like petroleum jelly and Vaseline? They wouldn't mean anything to him. They'd just sound like nonsense.

"He's peculiar about this new baby coming, too. Says he doesn't *need* a sister. I found him yesterday standing in the new crib with his pants down, peeing on the mattress. I can tell you he felt the back of my hand for *that* one.

"Honestly, I just don't have the strength. I'll be glad when she's finally born. Harvey keeps at me all the time to pick him up, and I just can't do it. 'Oh, Harvey,' I tell him, 'go on outdoors. Mommy's too tired. And you're getting to be a *big* boy now. Pretty soon there'll be a sweet new little baby to go in that crib.'

"I get so tired, but when I go to bed I can't sleep. So then the next day is even worse. And with Dave off in Seattle I have to do everything. It'll be better when he's finished up out there and can get home. I told him on the phone last night, 'Dave, you've gotta get back here and do something about Harvey. I just can't cope.' I told him about Harvey peeing in the crib and he just laughed. He said he was probably staking out his territory. Honestly!

"If I stay in any one position for too long I

get pins and needles all down my left leg. I said
to the doctor, I said, 'Now that's just not *right*!'
It really scared me. He said it was perfectly normal, some nerve was probably being pinched
with all that extra weight in there. Normal.
What would he know about it? Six kids he's got,
so he thinks he's an expert. It's his *wife* who's
the expert. It's her I should be talking to.

"I had some other things I wanted to ask
him, but with Harvey jumping on and off the
scales I couldn't concentrate, so I forgot them all
until I got home. Honestly, he drives me crazy.

"Tonight was the last straw. I sent him up
to get into his pyjamas and brush his teeth, and
I sat down to watch TV and work on my needle-
point. I've got this cute little lamb to go in the
baby's room, but at the rate I'm going it won't
be done in time. The lamb's in the centre,
that's the needlepoint part, and then you're
supposed to put the nursery rhyme, Mary had a
little lamb, all around the edges in embroidery.
I probably won't get to that. But the lamb by
itself will look okay. It's a real cute pattern.

"Anyway, I'm sitting there watching *Grace under Fire*, now *she* manages without a husband around, but that's on TV. Makes it all look funny. And she's got these supportive neighbours. All my neighbours do is complain about Harvey.

"Harvey. So he sneaks down the stairs and then leaps over the back of the couch, screaming at the top of his lungs. His head lands right on the lamb, and the needle sticks into his cheek. I'm so scared, and mad, I pick him up by the pyjama shirt to whack him and the buttons rip right off it. He's mad too, and he grabs a cushion from the couch and starts blubbering and hitting my stomach. Honestly, he's so violent! I don't know where he learns it.

"So now he's in bed, I carried him up there, even if he *is* too big to lift, I was that mad, and I threw him onto his bed and slammed the door.

"I've got to get off the phone. This chair's too hard, and anyway I'm waiting for Dave to call, boy is he going to get an earful to*night*! I can hear Harvey crying even though his door's shut, *god* that kid bugs me."

X MARKS THE SPOT

If the gap in the D minor scale provides the
opportunity to escape, to rise, to shake off the
humdrum and achieve epiphany, x is the
quicksand, the sinkhole, the sudden unexpected
suck down to axe murder. Something gone
wrong, sometimes horribly wrong.

Exorcize, exterminate, exhume. Exhale, for
the last time. Extinct. What elementary-school
child doesn't know that the way to indicate
death in a doodle-character (right in the margin
of the Geography textbook, beside the map
of South America) is to put an x in its eyeball?

Not that there isn't a certain fascination in-
herent in these downers. We've known at least
since Milton showed us, way back when, that evil
is more interesting than good, that smooth sail-
ing is a yawn. How many stories can you name,
about a treasure map and its alluring X, where
they dig and actually *find* anything? It's more
usual that they knife each other for the map,

or bash in each other's skulls with shovels when the chest is finally unearthed, or pry the chest open to find it empty or crawling with worms. Macabre variations on the Holy Grail story. To find it is to die; not to find it is still to die.

The first summer after we moved to Ontario, we rented a cottage. My dad lit a fire in the fireplace when we arrived, to take off the mustiness and chill. There were two square holes on either side of the stone chimney, covered with iron grills. A frantic mother mouse suddenly appeared through the smoke in one of them, holding a newborn baby mouse in her teeth. She poked it through the grill and it dropped the six feet to its death. Then another, and another, before my dad sprang into action and caught the rest of the litter in his hat. And then what? The mesh of the grill was too small to let the mother herself through. But I looked at the three tiny bodies on the floor and realized that dying was more than an x in the eyeball. Then my mind went on, as minds will, to list the exports of Paraguay.

Yarmouth to Bar Harbor

We got off the ferry on the fourth of July, my
mom and dad, my brother and I, in Bar Harbor,
Maine. Sea-salt and sunshine, wind, you could
almost drink the weather. There was a parade
on the main street, and we joined the crowd of
onlookers. My mom was originally from Ohio,
so she was thrilled to be part of this patriotic
scene.

When my dad was on, preaching a sermon,
say, or conducting a funeral, he was *really*
on. But when he got away his relaxation was
complete. So he was in his usual vacation mode:
baggy pants, an unbuttoned seersucker shirt,
and no dentures. The long strands of hair
growing in a clump at the front of his head,
which were combed back over his bald spot
when he entered the pulpit, were now braided
and tied in a knot. All in all, this was a version
of the charismatic preacher that few parish-
ioners were lucky enough to see.

As we watched the parade, he noticed a woman in the crowd who was in trouble. She had a baby in a carriage and a couple of toddlers, all three of them in tears. She needed to get them home, but home was across the float-filled street.

My dad may have taken out his teeth, but his sensibility was still in place. He stepped into the road, held up both arms, and brought the parade to a halt. Then he smiled at the woman, and she led her brood across. The crowd cheered, the parade resumed, my mother didn't know where to look.

. . .

My brother's first car was a Morris Minor convertible. He got it cheap because it had spent a couple of days submerged in the floodwaters of Hurricane Hazel. It didn't run very well, being full of silt, so he tore the engine apart in the driveway. I hunkered down on my heels to watch; sometimes I handed him tools.

"How do you know what you're doing?"
I asked him. He showed me the chart in the
manual: Exploded View of the Morris Minor
Engine. There was a drawing of each little
component, with a line to indicate where it had
come from (or where it was headed).

.   .   .

Like her father before her, my mother was a
diviner. A dowser. She could find water with a
forked stick. She told me this when I was little,
and, as always, I was skeptical. But one spring
day, when she was in her seventies, we went
walking in the woods. We came upon a cherry
tree and it put her in the mood. Willow is
best, she said, but cherry will do. So I cut a
forking branch. And sure enough, it worked.
Her arms trembled, her wrists turned, and her
eyes caught fire. She was *alive*, with an inten-
sity I'd never seen in her. I wish she'd shown
me earlier.

ZYMURGY

I drove my mom down to Ohio, to the sixtieth
anniversary of her graduation from university.
A much larger tale than I am going to tell
you here.

We took an afternoon off from the festivi-
ties and drove into Columbus to visit her best
friend from kindergarten. They had lived across
the street from each other, and walked
to school together.

"Your mother," the woman said to me,
"was always too busy to clean her fingernails.
So when I'd knock on her door in the mornings
she'd be cramming talcum powder under her
nails to keep the dirt from showing."

The two of them, in their eighties, laughing
about being five years old. Their stories were
so compelling, they inhabited the past with
such vigour, that I began to feel insubstantial.
My god, what am I doing here? I haven't been
born yet. The ghost of things to come.

The woman's husband was also there, sitting in his wheelchair, unable to speak. He and I contented ourselves with indulgent smiles while the giggling continued. I looked across the room to a set of bookcases, and there on the bottom shelf was the two-volume dictionary of my childhood.

"Hey," I said, "there's *A to pocketveto* and *Pockmark to zymurgy and supplements*!" When I was seven I took a great deal of satisfaction in saying "and supplements." Here's everything, and then here's the rest of it.

The old man was amazed and then delighted that I'd recognized the volumes and knew their names from memory. He beamed. I'd made his day. One of the most gratifying pieces of cheering up I've ever done. I'm smiling about it now, as I write, and he's long since gone to his grave.

Zymurgy: "That branch of chemistry which deals with the process of fermentation, as in wine-making, brewing, distilling, the preparation of yeast."

Organizing a piece of writing around the alphabet isn't as artificial and facile as it may at first appear. The sequence of letters encompasses the whole territory of what we are able to utter. Crabapples, beans, malapropisms, the dying mice. The dear sweet boy, tucking up his baby sister in her suck-thumb blanket. And then there's poor small Harvey, with little hope of a contented life.

What do we do with it all? How do we take in this teeming geography? We can only look around us, discover the things we care about, and cherish them.

A typo in "Penny," *quatrer*, and the spell checker suggests "quatrain." He obviously wasn't paying attention to the story. Probably off having a beer with Fred, watching him make macaroons. Fred's become quite the chef.

But it's an interesting idea to throw into the mix. Who occupies this space on the page? Is it the writer, or the narrator, or a fictitious "I/eye" of their invention? And who's the landlord? Absentee or live-in? What makes this ultimately hang together? *Some*body has to pay the utility bills. And look after babies; the dramatis personae is overrun with babies. The producer has his hands full. The props list is staggering. The crabapples start to rot; the Inuit complain, understandably, of the heat; baby's breath, as we all know, is hard to come by. The clock, still unassembled, is spread out on the table. Will this whole crazy thing ever fly?

I'm tired. My brain has been vacuumed dry. There's so much going on. I missed most of what happened yesterday; I'll only catch part of tomorrow. I got them started, they seem to be on a roll, I can hear Harvey's mom complaining to Dave, who's finally back from Seattle. Somebody's got hold of a case of macaroons, and is doing trial runs with a car. Some stick, some don't. The Dingbats are flicking their switchblades into the casting board. The metaphors lounge on the comforters, chewing on the green beans. Mrs. Tiggy-Winky Malaprop's voice calls out over the hubbub, *I don't mean to cry your river.*

I leave them all wringing their hands and come out on the back porch with a beer. Full moon, crickets. I hum a D minor scale into the darkness. There may be frost by morning.

Acknowledgements

I'm grateful to the other members of my
writing group, Claudette Guthrie and Kathie
Lambert, for their sustaining enthusiasm;

to George Sipos, who reads with exquisite care;

and to Barbara Pulling, my editor at Douglas
& McIntyre, for her good eye, her amiable
editing style, and for indulging me in my
"grammatical weirdnesses."

I'm indebted to the Canada Council for
furnishing me with the time to complete
this book.

JEAN McKAY